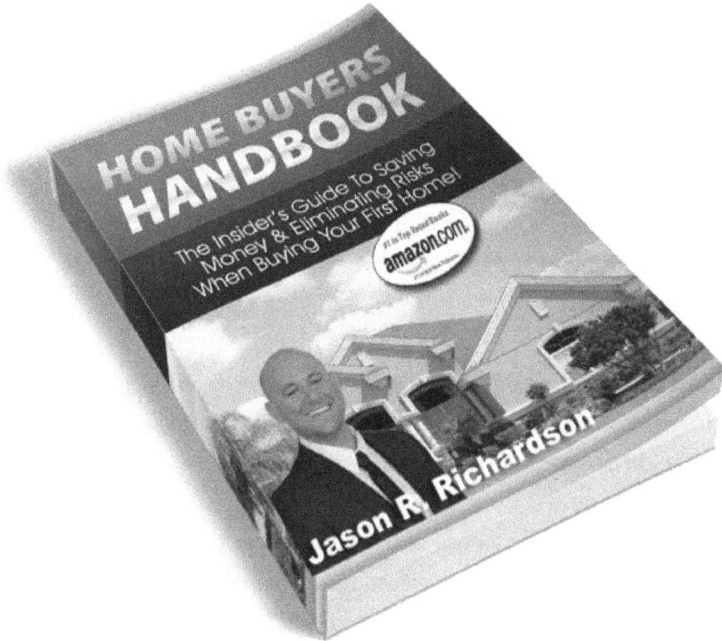

The Mortgage Geek

Home Buyers Handbook

www.JasonRRichardson.com

LEGAL NOTICE

Table of Contents

Introduction

You're at the point in your life where you're seriously considering purchasing your first home. You're sick of paying high rental costs when you know that you'll never own that property and it simply makes sense to start investing in your own future.

Buying a home is an exciting adventure, and whether this is your first home or your second, it's important that you take your time when evaluating potential properties so that you end up with a property that truly reflects your style, your preferences, your lifestyle and of course, the size of your family.

When considering properties, you also need to think outside of just the property itself. While that Cape Code on the corner may look like your dream home, what about the neighborhood?

The property costs in certain divisions? Are land taxes reasonable? Are you responsible for water charges? Sewer charges? Recycling costs?

Are there any zoning regulations or restrictions that you should be aware of?

You should also consider your own personal lifestyle and make sure that the neighborhood is reflective of where you are in your life and what you are comfortable with.

For instance, perhaps you're retired and looking to settle down in a quiet, mature neighborhood only to discover that the majority of families around you are all younger couples, with small children. It's important to look at the big picture when choosing a property so that it truly offers you the setting and the atmosphere that you are most comfortable with. After all, this is your home and you are going to spend many years building a life there!

Driving by a property isn't enough, and even if you love the layout, structure and design of a home, there are outside factors that should influence your decision to buy.

Some of these things may include:

- Choosing a neighborhood reflective of your own lifestyle.
- Considering the layout of a home (open concept, 3 story, etc)
- Considering the size of the property and whether there is room to expand.
- Choosing a property with adequate privacy.
- Choosing a property with a backyard, trees or fencing.
- Choosing a property that offers features most important to you.
- Whether the property needs improvements (and costs associated)
- Evaluating the different real estate companies available to you.
- Understanding zoning regulations, the housing market, additional costs.

There are other factors to consider outside of the property itself as well, so that you can purchase a home with limited risk s involved, including:

- Hiring a home inspection company.
- Financing opportunities, mortgages, and loans.
- How to put in your first offer.
- Setting a closing date that works for you and the seller.
- Understanding contracts, hiring a real estate attorney.
- Moving expenses, hiring a moving company
- Closing the deal and moving in!

There are many things to keep in mind when buying a home, and if it's your first time purchasing a property, it can become overwhelming. Rest assured, that your real estate broker and attorney will take care of many of these things, but you want to take a hands on approach when evaluating properties and considering your options so that you can get the best deal possible.

One of the biggest mistakes that new home buyers make is rushing into a deal. They see a property that they absolutely love. It's perfect! The size, privacy, layout – it's everything they could hope for only to find out that the property needs repairs, or that the land taxes are higher than in a neighboring town.

So, it's important that you keep an open mind when evaluating potential houses, and take your time! There are always other homes that could fit your lifestyle and personal preferences, so if you find one that has potential problems, move on!

Careful planning and thorough research will help you make the transition into your new home easier (and more affordable) than if you rush into an offer, or make a last minute decision on a property, so give yourself adequate time to visit properties before you even begin your search.

If you are currently renting and are considering giving notice to your landlord, make sure that you feel comfortable with the allocated time in finding a new home.

Depending on your area, you may be required to give your landlord 60-90 days notice, so keep that in mind so that you don't accrue additional expenses by having to pay for rent when you are no longer there.

When beginning your search for a home, you want to consider all options so that you can get the best deal possible. This includes:

New Homes vs. Older Homes

Older homes can be more affordable; however you may also be faced with costly repairs, such as replacing old equipment so that it's up to code. Older homes often carry higher insurance rates because of an increased risk of repairs.

On the other hand, older homes can make for great starter houses, if you have the ability to do a lot of the repairs yourself. And in many cases, you can end up buying a larger house at a fraction of the cost in comparison with a newer home.

In addition, many people prefer mature properties because of the history surrounding the property, as well as existing vegetation, trees, and greenery, which provides privacy, while often giving buyers the opportunity to purchase more land for future development, than with a newer model.

But there are many pro's and con's to both a new and older home and it's important that you fully understand everything about the properties that you are considering. Get as much history on the property as possible.

Ask the realtor for information about the home, talk to neighbors, check out sale history by searching online.

Reviewing the history of sale transactions on a home can often give you a good idea as to whether there were problems with the property, especially if it's been sold multiple times over a short period of time.

Also keep in mind that newer homes include a warranty, protecting you from unforeseen costs in repairs (such as roofing or flooring), while older homes will typically be sold "as is."

When purchasing an older home, you want to make sure that you pay an inspection company to thoroughly inspect the property, including roofing, heating, electrical outlets, and whether the property is up to code including the type of wiring found throughout the property.

While it's important to have a home inspection on both new and older homes, if the property is aged, you will want to make sure the inspection includes elements that may not be typically included in an inspection process for a newer home.

Moving into your new home should be an exciting and memorable time in your life, and if you really give yourself enough time to evaluate different properties, and you keep an open mind with both newer and older homes, you'll be in a better position to get the most 'bang for your buck', while ending up with a home that you are happy with for years to come.

Chapter 1 – Location Is Everything

One of the greatest factors in regards to overall costs of property is in the neighborhood or area itself.

In real estate, **location is everything** and depending on what your personal preferences are, you should expect the costs of properties to change based on location, even when all other features and factors are similar.

For example, if you choose to live just outside of a city zone, a property of the same age and size could be as much as $50,000 cheaper than a property inside of a city zone.

You will also want to consider what is available in different areas, based on what is most important to you. Are there grocery stores local to the neighborhoods you are evaluating? Are there late night conveniences? Entertainment? Doctors? Schools?

All of these factors will influence your decision to buy within certain areas, and if you have small children, you'll also want to consider the quality of the schools in the same way that if you require regular medical treatment, you'll want to make sure that there are medical facilities near your home.

For many homebuyers, location is the most important component when choosing a property and it's also the key factor in which they spend the most time evaluating. You want the conveniences that are of most importance to you!

If you are considering purchasing a property outside of a city zone based on the savings, you'll also want to make sure that the lower property rate is justified based on the costs to commute.

On the other hand, if you are interested in living within city limits, you will want to pay attention to additional costs and factors such as metered water, sewage costs, pet restrictions and any by-laws that you may be affected by.

For example, in many cities there are bylaws preventing residents from having too many pets, and believe it or not, there are even bylaws that indicate what color you can paint your home!

So be careful in choosing a neighborhood just based on cost alone. You will want to discuss any bylaws or restrictions applied to an area with your realtor before making an offer on a property.

When considering different locations, you will want to try to spend some time in each area, so that you are able to get a personal feel for the neighborhood.

Consider staying in a nearby bed & breakfast or a hotel for a weekend, so that you can explore the area, walk through the neighborhoods, visit nearby attractions, restaurants, parks, and even speak with the locals.

While many people overlook this simple step, it can really make a difference in helping you choose an area where you feel safe, relaxed and truly connected to.

If you have children, you will also want to include them in making your decision. Spend some family time around the different areas that you are considering so that there are few surprises when you move in.

Pay attention the proximity of nearby schools, whether there are local events for your children based on their interests, whether you will be close to amenities or areas that you'll visit frequently, and whether you can really see yourself living in an area for a long period of time.

When considering whether to purchase a home in the country, city or suburbs, weigh the pros and cons of all three areas, to gain a better idea as to what is suitable for your family.

City living carries many different benefits, including:

- Quick & Easy access to local events.
- Extended business hours for many different amenities.
- More options for stores, restaurants and schools.
- Public transportation.
- Typically offers more cultural events, concerts, attractions.

Just the same, there are also cons to living in the city as well, including:

- Higher population.
- Less property.
- Higher housing costs.
- Higher taxes.
- Higher crime rate.
- Higher pollution rate.
- Limiting housing available.

If considering buying a house in the country, you will also want to weigh the pros and cons including:

Pros:

- More property available.
- Lower tax costs.
- Less population.
- Not as many zoning issues or bylaws.

- Overall cost of living is lower.

Cons:

- Fewer amenities available.
- Further commute to work and shopping.
- Fewer schools & businesses to choose from.
- Issues dealing with wells, septic systems, etc.
- Less entertainment, cultural events.

Other Location Considerations

- Weather & Climate
- Road conditions
- Location of property in the neighborhood, and
- Room to expand

You should be thinking ahead in terms of the weather. If you are planning on living in the country, for example, you should pay attention to possible flooding, snow, and other weather that could affect you getting to work.

If the road is a dirt road, you should ask if the county will clear the road and how often they will do so. This is another advantage of living in the city because you could always use public transportation if you do not want to drive.

The location of the property is also important. If the property is located at the bottom of a slope, you may have flooding issues after a rainstorm. Also, as your family grows, you may need more room.

You should find property that can hold a home addition if necessary. Investing in a home requires a great deal of thought and planning. Even if you do not have a family, you should find a home that will allow you to grow as your interests change.

If you are planning on taking out a mortgage, you will find it difficult to move abruptly in the event you discover that an area isn't quite what you expected, so the more time you spend personally evaluating the neighborhoods and areas you are interested in, the more prepared you will be to make an informed decision.

Another important thing to keep in mind is the crime rate of specific areas. You can identify and potential problems or higher crime rates by researching areas online. You can also talk to your realtor about any concerns you have over crime rates, and make sure to compare crime rates to other neighborhoods.

You also want to pay attention to your 'gut instinct' and how you personally feel about an area, when it comes to choosing a property:

Does a certain neighborhood give you a sense of calm? Does it provoke a positive feeling? Good memories? Does it seem clean and friendly?

And depending on your lifestyle, you will also want to pay attention to other contributing factors including:

- Is there high speed Internet available?
- Is there cable television available?
- Are there ponds, rivers, lakes or oceans nearby?
- Are there 24-hour conveniences? (drug stores, grocery stores, etc)
- Is the neighborhood aesthetically pleasing?
- Is there garbage pickup?
- What is the average value of a home in that neighborhood?

All of these things will play a part in helping you to decide whether a specific property is suitable for your family, so take the time to research the different locations and start taking notes regarding your findings.

Having this information readily available will provide you with a snapshot of the different properties and locations that you are considering, making it easier to come to a decision later on.

Chapter 2 – Finding a Realtor

If you are like many people, chances are that you've looked around different neighborhoods, saw a few homes that were for sale, maybe visited an open house or two, and then felt stuck.

What is the next step? Approach the homeowner with a potential offer? Visit a realtor for more information and help with the purchase?

Finding the right realtor when buying a home depends on what you are looking for in a home. You may have to visit several realtors before finding one that listens to your wants and needs.

After all, you will probably be paying them a commission once you have found a home, so you should be comfortable working with them during the house hunting process.

Choosing A Realtor

There are a few ways to find a reliable realtor. For example, you can:

- Ask friends and family for referrals.
- Search online for approved realtors.
- Attend a few open houses and meet realtors personally.
- Visit a local real estate office, or
- Look for local realtors in your neighborhood by paying attention to for sale signs in the neighborhood

Asking plenty of questions before looking at houses may seem like a lot of work, but when you visit a realtor for the first time, you should think about questions that will help you get to know this person who is going to help you find your dream home. The five best questions to ask are:

1. Are you a certified realtor?
2. How long have you been in the real estate business?
3. Which neighborhoods are you the most familiar with?
4. How many homes do you have that will fit my needs?
5. What is your typical commission on a home in my price range?

Once you have asked these questions, you should be looking for honest and complete answers, good communication, and honesty. These are questions that the realtor should have practice in answering and should not have to give you a standard 'salesperson' answer.

If you feel uncomfortable, remember that you are under no obligation to continue with this realtor unless they have some good property matches to show you, or have exclusive rights to show properties that you are interested in.

Normally, if a realtor does not have properties that fit what you are looking for, they will recommend you to another realtor in the group. This is also a good sign because it shows that the group is looking out for your interests and the interests of its employees.

You should also pay attention to:

- How well your realtor listens to what you are looking for
- How well they understand current real estate law
- How many other clients they seem to have
- How they speak to their co workers
- How often they communicate with you on the phone or email

In the end, you will have to be the judge of the real estate agent. If they know what they are talking about, can find out the information you need quickly, and are willing to take the time to listen to what you need, then you should work very well with them.

In some cases, you may be asked to sign an agreement that states you will only be working with a specific real estate agency or agent when looking for a home. You are under no obligation to sign this paperwork and you should only do so if you feel very comfortable.

While these agreements are not totally binding, it could make buying a home more difficult down the road. Only sign agreements if you feel comfortable.

During your search for a real estate agent, you will find a variety of agents that will want to work with you. These include:

- Experienced agents
- New agents
- Pushy agents
- Absentee agents, and
- Hard working agents

While all real estate agents have different personalities, you will have to decide which ones you will want to work with when looking for your new home.

Experienced Agents vs. New Agents

This is an age old debate that should be addressed. While an experienced agent may have sold more homes and earned more commissions, new agents can be just as helpful and need to get some sales under their belt, which may prompt them to work harder for you.

While you should ask about their experience, you should take into consideration other traits such as the ability to listen and the ability to only show you homes in your price range.

Experienced agents and new agents have been trained in a similar fashion and only have their personalities to bring to the table.

There are experienced agents out there who will drag their feet because they are over confident or they are not as interested in their jobs as they once were. Experienced agents may know more about different neighborhoods, but some of them are not as proactive as they used to be.

You should not let inexperience deter you when looking for an agent. Many times new agents will work harder because they want to gain a reputation that they can use to build confidence in their future clients

Pushy Agents

Unfortunately, you will meet real estate agents that will want to sell you more home than you need. In an effort to earn larger commissions or to sell those properties that are more difficult, many agents will try this tactic.

This is where you will need to stand firm. You do not want to waste your time looking at homes that are beyond your price range unless you can find a way to lower the price.

While looking at possible homes is exciting, this will not last long as you will grow weary of spending all of your available time looking for a home. If an agent keeps showing you homes that are out of your price range, then you should consider finding another agent.

Absentee Agents

Absentee real estate agents are those agents who show you a few homes and then disappear for a few weeks. These agents may be overworked, may not be able to find a home in your price range or neighborhood, or have higher priced commissions to find. Whatever the reasons, this is unprofessional behavior and should be rectified immediately, especially if you need to find a home quickly.

If an agent does not have homes in your price range or neighborhood, they should recommend another agent in the group. Agencies never want to lose customers. If your agent does not do this, find a new one.

Even agents that are overworked have time to make a quick phone call. If you do not hear from your agent in a week after your last meeting, find another agent.

Hard Working Agents

These are the best agents to find when you are buying your first home. If you find an agent like this one, do not lose them. These are the agents that will follow every lead, pass your wants and needs to another agent, and try their best to find you a home. You should expect to see a handful of homes when working with an agent like this one.

Now that you know more about what to look for in a real estate agent, you should feel a little more comfortable about working with one. They can be an invaluable source of information when you want to know more about homes, neighborhoods, and other questions about the communities you are looking at.

When looking at homes with your real estate agent, you should ask questions about the home, the neighborhood, the city or town, and any other questions you need to know in order to make an informed decision. Part of your real estate agents job is to research homes and neighborhoods so that they can answer questions that may come up.

Preparing To See Homes With Your Realtor

Create A List

Once you have found a realtor you are comfortable with, you will want to make the most of your time when house hunting. Giving your realtor a list of what you are looking for will help narrow the search and save everyone some time. Your list should include:

- Your price range
- Number of bedrooms you want
- Number of bathrooms
- Size of property
- Basement (finished or unfinished)
- If you want a porch, patio or balcony
- Central heat and air conditioning
- Garage
- Neighborhood, and
- Any other amenities you would like

Giving your real estate agent a list of your preferences will allow them to spend more time researching homes that fit the criteria. You should list these amenities from greatest to least important because no home is perfect and you will not get everything you want or need. Let your agent know that you are flexible, but that you really want to concentrate on certain items when looking for a home.

Viewing Homes

When looking at homes with your agent, be sure to ask any questions you may have. While these questions may seem small, they may be important to your happiness. Common questions people ask their agents are:

- How old is the home?
- How many owners has the home had?
- What kinds of renovations have been done to the home?
- How old is the plumbing?
- How low are the sellers willing to go?
- How old is the carpeting and flooring?
- How old are the windows?

While your agent may answer some of these questions before you ask them, you should ask any questions that may influence your decision to buy a home. If you do not want to put too much work into fixing up the home, you may want to buy a home that is ten years old or less.

If your agent does not know all of the answers to your questions, they should be able to find out and will give you an answer within a day or two.

Taking Pictures

One of the best ways to remember the homes you have seen is to bring your camera or take pictures with your phone. Get permission from the agent first before taking pictures of another person's home.

Many times, after looking at a few houses, you will forget how big the kitchen in home number two was in comparison to home number five. Having pictures will give you a better idea of the square footage and how much room you will have to work with.

Narrowing Down Your Choices

After a few weeks of viewing homes that fit what you are looking for, you should be close to finding a home that you will want to make a bid on. If you have other homes you would like to see or you have changed your mind as to what you are looking for, you should tell your agent so that they can look for other homes.

Many times, if a person likes the neighborhood but not the home they were shown, they will want to see other homes in the neighborhood that are for sale. You should ask to see all of the homes available in a neighborhood that you like.

If you are still not finding a home that you like, you may need to change the neighborhoods you are looking at. While this can seem disappointing, your real estate agent will be happy to show you homes in different neighborhoods. Sometimes if you compare homes to one another, you will find redeeming qualities in a home you have already seen.

Once you have found a home that you like, you should make an offer. Contact your agent as soon as you can so that they can draw up the paperwork, contact the buyer's agent, and make an offer before another person does. Make an offer as soon as you can in order to avoid a bidding war.

Bidding can be long and drawn out in some cases. If you do not have the time to wait out a bid or if you cannot bid any higher, then you may be looking for another home to purchase. While this can set you back, you should try to stay positive and find a home that is right for you.

Your agent should be there to guide you along during this time. Ask all the questions you have to before making an offer on a home.

Information Realtors Should Tell You

There is plenty of information that realtors can tell you about the homes you will be viewing. Things they should tell you include:

- The price of the home
- The age of the home
- Any renovations that have been done
- Any other Issues with the home
- Property taxes
- Community dues
- Schools
- Neighborhood crime rates, and
- The median age of those who live in the neighborhood

Usually, if a realtor does not have the information you request on hand, they will be able to look it up once they are back at their office.

You should be able to find out all the information you need to know in order to make an informed decision about buying a home. Realtors are required by law to give you information concerning repairs, damage, and the history of a home.

This includes any incidents that have occurred inside the home such as criminal activity, fire, and other events.

You can also do a little research of your own by using the Internet, which has become a wonderful tool to use when searching for a home. You can research past events that have taken place in the neighborhood, the home itself, or the town where you want to live. Knowing a little history may prompt you to look elsewhere or make an offer.

Other information realtors can tell you include:

- Home owner price reduction (your realtor will talk with the seller's realtor once you have made an offer or want to make an offer to see how low the owners will go to sell the home)
- Prices of other homes in the area that are comparable to the one you are looking into buying
- How quickly the owner wants or needs to sell their home
- How much you will have to pay in property taxes each year, on average
- Other taxes in the area

Your realtor is a person that should be well acquainted with the neighborhoods you are looking at when buying your first home. Don't be afraid to ask many questions.

Working With Seller's And Buyer's Agents

As a home buyer, your real estate agent is considered the buyer's agent. While some people will forego hiring an agent at first when looking for a home in order to save money on commission costs, they will usually end up hiring an agent to:

- Handle negotiations with sellers
- Do paperwork, and
- Survey neighborhoods

It is in your best interest to hire an agent in order to make buying a home a much easier, and faster process.

Negotiations With Sellers

Most people who sell their homes are also working with an agent. This agent is known as a seller's agent. If you choose not to hire an agent, you will be dealing with a seller's agent who is looking out for the home owner's interests, and not yours.

Sometimes, though, the seller's agent and the buyer's agent can be the same agent. This means that your agent is looking after the interests of everyone involved. This is a rare occurrence, and it is best to hire a real estate agent that can negotiate with other agents in order to get you the best deal on a home.

Negotiating with agents can take a week or more depending on how high you are willing to go and how low the owners are willing to go. This can become a complicated game once you introduce home inspectors.

After an initial home inspection, if you feel there are repairs that should be made prior to the sale of the home, or if you want a price reduction because of the repairs you will have to make, you will have to negotiate with the owners to settle on a fair price. Without an agent, you will have to do all of this work yourself.

Paperwork

When buying a home, there is a lot of paperwork that must be completed before the closing. This paperwork can include:

- Offers
- Counteroffers
- Home inspection reports
- Home appraisal reports, and

- Fixture lists (Items that come with the home and items you would like removed)

Filing the paperwork is not difficult, but it can take some time. Working with an agent will save you time and money when creating and sending out paperwork.

Survey Neighborhoods

Another advantage to hiring an agent is that you will not have to do as much legwork in the beginning. You may have a few neighborhoods in mind, but you will be able to leave it to your agent to find homes for sale and setting up appointments to see them.

This is another time saver especially if you have to work during the week. Taking time from your busy day to call other agents and homeowners to set up appointments will distract you from your other daily duties.

More Reasons To Hire A Real Estate Agent

There are several other reasons to hire a real estate agent. These include:

Peace Of Mind

The bottom line is that as a buyer, a buyer's agent is the best resource when it comes to finding and making an offer on a home. While a seller's agent will be able to tell you the basics about a home, they are working for the homeowner.

They will not try to get you the lowest price for the home.

If you enjoy negotiating, then working with seller's agents might be for you. But if you are like most people, hiring an agent to work on your side will make the entire process more enjoyable and worthwhile in the end.

Wealth Of Knowledge

Your agent will be very knowledgeable about negotiating the right price for your new home, they will be able to help you decide where you want to live, and they will be able to guide you in buying or walking away from any property you are not sure about. This is why it is so important to talk with your agent and ask as many questions as you can before buying a home.

Confidence

If you are having doubts about purchasing the home you have made an offer on, then you should tell your agent right away so that they can postpone the offer made and help you reexamine what it is you are looking for in a home. Many times the initial shock of being a homeowner can be overwhelming.

Sometimes talking with your agent is enough to resolve your feelings. Other times, you may need to see a few more homes before making a decision. Your agent will be able to give you practical advice during this time.

Chapter 3 – Watching the Market

Now that you know more about finding a real estate agent, you should begin watching the housing market carefully in the weeks or months before buying your first home in order to get a feel for whether it is in your favor.

Watching The Housing Market

For the past year, the housing market has been favoring buyers. Soaring market values were short-lived as many people decided they just could not afford to live in certain areas because of the cost of housing.

This has caused many sellers to lower their prices. While this sounds like good news for you, the housing market can be very fickle.

Depending on where you want to live, you may end up having to pay a small fortune for the home of your dreams.

This is why watching the market, surveying neighborhoods, and finding a good agent will help you in your search.

While you should not become a slave to the housing market, you should keep the following in mind before buying your first home:

- The past market value of the home you are interested in buying
- How much house your budget can get you in different neighborhoods and towns
- Neighborhood value
- How much the home should increase over time, and
- Price reductions that may be available

Just because you buy a home for a great deal does not mean you will make a huge profit when it is time to sell it. The housing market will continue to change and since this is your first home, you may want to choose something you can pay off quickly and make a larger profit on in the future.

Also, remember that any improvements you make on the home will increase its overall value. Just don't spend too much money on improvements. Creating a home improvement budget and sticking with it will help you make those monthly mortgage payments and other payments that will be due.

One of the biggest mistakes that first time homeowners can make is buying a home for a lot less than they budgeted and then making improvements that will end up costing more money in the end. If you can find a great deal on a home, use that extra money as a cushion in case you lose your job or are too ill to work.

Owning a home is a big responsibility. Knowing how the market is moving and spending your money wisely will help when you are creating a budget, applying for a mortgage, and deciding how much to put down on a home.

Making The Most Of The Housing Market

While you should be watching the housing market, there are other areas of interest you should be watching also, such as:

- National interest rates for mortgages
- Building rates in your area
- Number of foreclosures in your area, and
- Stock market and gasoline prices

National Interest Rates For Mortgages

Even though the housing market may be going your way does not mean that the interest rates you could be paying are. In the times when the housing market has taken a slump, interest rates tend to rise in order to retain the natural balance within the economy.

The interest rate you receive will depend on many factors, including:

- Other loans
- Current credit score
- Credit history
- Number of credit cards
- Yearly income
- Owed debts
- Current interest rates
- Type of lender
- Time of year, and
- Adjustable and fixed rate mortgage

If you see housing prices dropping, you may opt to buy a larger home than you would have if the prices had been higher a year ago. While you will be saving money on that end, you may be paying more each month because of the interest rate you received.

Building Rates In Your Area

If you notice the housing market has also caused the building of new homes in your area to decrease, then you may have to enter into a bidding war in order to buy your first home. When new home construction goes down, this can mean one of several things:

- The area is no longer popular
- The interest in buying a new home has diminished
- People can no longer afford to purchase new homes
- People are opting for older homes that are less expensive to heat and keep cool during the year

While that housing slump may bring a reduction of housing prices, you should consider making a bid soon after finding the home of your dreams because bidding wars will only end up costing your more money.

Number Of Foreclosures In Your Area

When looking for a home, you should consider looking at homes that are under foreclosure. This can be for many reasons, but usually banks that hold the titles want to unload these homes quickly so that they do not lose more money than necessary. Many times auctions will be held or the home will be advertised as a foreclosure in the newspaper or online.

You should check out these homes because you may find exactly what you are looking for in a home.

Stock Market And Gasoline Prices

Even if you do not play the stock market game or own a car, you should still pay attention to these areas because they are usually what will dictate housing prices and the cost to heat and cool the home.

When the stock market is doing well many people will spend their money more freely, which will give way to higher housing prices. But when gasoline prices go up so will the price to heat and cool a home, which may make homebuyers reconsider buying until the prices fall again.

This could be a good time to buy a home if you are willing to pay a little more each month in utility costs.

The impact society can have on the housing market can be huge, and it can also have lasting effects. Buyer's markets are created when there are more homes available than buyers, while seller's market occurs when there are more people who want to purchase homes than there are for sale. These housing markets go back and forth due to issues mentioned above.

In The End

Buy a home when you are ready. Many times, people will buy a home because it is cheaper in the long run than paying rent each month.

The downside to home ownership is that you have to make your mortgage payments on time each month. Very few lenders will give you more time to come up with the money.

If you miss even one payment, your home could be foreclosed upon. You will have no place to live and your credit score will suffer severely.

If you can afford to make the move into your new home now, you should not wait too long before making an offer. The housing market can change quickly and with competition out there, you may end up losing more money if you don't make an offer after seeing a home that you like.

Rent To Own

Another option you may have is to buy the property you are currently renting or rent a property that also offers you the option to buy after a certain amount of time. This will give you a chance to see if you like living in the home and will give you time to get your finances in order.

Rent to own properties are usually older than other homes and have been rental properties for some time. This means that they may not be in great shape. If you are looking for a property that you don't mind repairing, then this option may be for you.

When looking at a rent to own property, you should ask the following questions:

- How old is the home?
- How many times has it been rented out?
- What is the mortgage payment on the home?
- What is the rent per month for the home?
- How long will I have to make my decision?
- What happens if I change my mind?
- What happens if the home owner changes their mind?

You should still sign the proper contracts stating that you are interested in buying the home after the given time period. This will protect your rights and the rights of the current homeowner.

New Homes

When you think of your first home, you may be thinking of a brand new home. Since the housing market is favoring buyers at the moment, you may get a great deal from a builder that is developing a new housing community, or you may find a plot of land that is in an existing community. This can be a great alternative to buying an older home for many reasons:

- You will have a part in designing the home
- You will have new appliances and lighting fixtures
- You will have new carpeting and flooring
- You will be able to choose all of the fixtures, carpeting, and flooring
- You will be able to add a porch or a patio, and
- You will be able to place the home where you want it on your property

A new home can be very exciting, but it can also be a lot of extra work. The first step in buying a new home is to find property. You should visit builders and real estate agents who will file all of the necessary paperwork, permits, and other items needed to build on the property. This can take a few weeks, so be sure to plan accordingly.

The next step is to design the home. This is the fun part where you will get to personalize your home to suit your needs.

Once you have been approved for a mortgage, the property has passed all of the land inspections, and the home has been designed, construction will begin. Depending on the time of year, you will have to wait about three months before you can move into your new home.

After construction is complete, you should complete a walkthrough of the home, check all of the fixtures, and have the home inspected before signing the final paperwork. Then the home is yours.

Many people hire a lawyer during the construction phase so that all of the paperwork has been filed and there are no problems during the walk through.

Buying a new home is just one more option you should consider when looking for your first home. Home construction can vary, as there are a few ways to build a home, including pre-fab homes that will be built elsewhere and delivered to your property where they will be assembled. Look into all of your options before deciding on a home that is right for you and your budget.

Using The Housing Market To Your Advantage

By paying attention to current housing trends and keeping a watchful eye on the homes in your area, you will be able to make an offer on a home that will be accepted.

While the market is continually changing, it is a useful tool for those who are on a budget, who want to find a home that is large enough to suit their needs, and will be worth more when it is time to sell it.

When watching the housing market, consider the following:

- The number of homes that are in your area
- The number of days the homes have been on the market
- The price of a new home compared to those that are being sold by homeowners
- The price of renting vs. buying
- The number of homes that are in your price range

- The highest price you can pay when buying a home
- Interest rates in comparison to housing prices, and
- The time of year

Springtime is a good time to buy a home for several reasons:

- More people want to sell
- It is easier to make appointments to view homes
- Prices are usually lower
- People are more willing to reduce their asking price
- Income tax returns can help with a buyer's budget

There will be plenty of people who could not sell their homes in the fall or winter months and who are trying to sell before the summertime. Homeowners that need to sell their homes before a certain time are more willing to reduce the price of their homes.

While you should consider looking at a home during any time of the year, you will find that many homes will be lower in the spring to attract buyers.

This is also the time when interest rates are re-evaluated and many lenders are willing to give loans to those whose credit is not the best. Take advantage of when interest rates are at their lowest even if it means accepting an adjustable rate mortgage. You will have the option of locking into a fixed rate at a later time.

While the housing market can change, the idea of selling one's home will not. Homeowners may choose to wait out the current housing market, but if they are eager to buy another home or move to a new place, their wait will be short-lived.

Negotiate with homeowners until a fair price can be reached. This is the same practice during a seller's market as in a buyer's market. You may have to play the bidding game for a week or two, but in the end, it is the person who needs to make the transaction happen the most that will end up compromising the most.

Chapter 4 – Home Inspections 101

A home inspection will give you a chance to discover more about the home before you purchase it. In case there are serious problems with the foundation, mold issues, or underground leaks, you will be prepared to ask for repairs, a reduced price, or walk away from the property.

The Importance Of Home Inspections

Finding a home does not mean that your investigative duties are over. Although most states do not have required inspections, your lender may require at the very least a pest inspection that will need to be conducted before they agree to approve your mortgage loan. If there are termites or other insects, the home owners will have to take care of the problem before they sell the home.

But what about full home inspections? Are they worth it? In most cases, the answer is yes. Although you will have to pay for a home inspection, it may save you a lot of money in the long run.

A thorough home inspection will include checking the following:

- Electrical systems
- Heating and cooling systems
- Foundation
- Siding
- Structural elements
- Roof
- Insulation
- Doors and windows, and
- Plumbing

If you are buying a new or used home, it is best to have a home inspection before signing the final paperwork. Once the inspection report comes back, you will the opportunity to ask the homeowners for a price reduction, go ahead and buy the home anyway, or ask the homeowners to make the necessary repairs.

You will receive a varied reaction from homeowners. Many times, they will agree to lower the price a little.

When drawing up an initial offer for the purchase of the home, you should include a statement that allows you to withdraw your bid if any repairs are not taken care of or the price is not lowered due to the findings by the home inspector.

If the contract does not include this, then you can still withdraw from the bid, but you still may owe fees.

Having a home inspection will give you peace of mind when you are buying a home. Since you will be taking out a mortgage, it is important to know what you will be buying, and the amount of money you will have to invest after purchasing the home.

A home inspection will also help you make your final decision whether to purchase the home or to keep looking for another.

How To Find A Home Inspector

There are a few places to turn to when looking for a home inspector:

- Your real estate agent
- References from friends and family
- The phone book, and
- Contractors

Ask around and see if you can get references of other homeowners that will give you a good report. Many home inspectors work freelance and only work certain days during the week. They are trained in home inspection and many are retired contractors, builders, electricians, and plumbers who know what they are looking for.

When you find a few home inspectors, give them a call and ask the following questions:

- How long have you been inspecting homes?
- How much do you charge per hour?
- What do you look for when inspecting a home?
- What types of reports should I expect?
- What days during the week are you available?
- Do you offer septic system inspections?
- What type of licensing do you have?

A thorough home inspection should take an inspector about three hours to complete. This will give you an idea of how much the inspection will cost.

Once you have asked these questions, find out if your lender has specific inspections that the home must pass before you will receive a home loan.

 If the inspector can complete these inspections along with the home inspection, then it is worth the time and the money to have the inspector complete all inspections on the same day.

The next step after choosing an inspector and finding out which inspections will be needed by your lender is to make sure the homeowners will be home for the inspection. Usually your agent will arrange a time for the inspector to perform the inspection.

It is up to you if you would like to be present for the inspection or not. Many times, the reports will be enough to give you a clear idea of what needs to be done. After the inspection is complete and the reports have been completed, it is up to the homeowners to either make the repairs necessary or lower their asking price.

If the repairs are minor and will not require too much money to repair, they will usually agree to make the repairs. If you would like to absorb the costs of the repairs, then you can offer to do so.

You should receive this decision in writing so that there is no confusion during the final walk through before the closing. At the closing, you should have all of your paperwork, including the home inspection reports with you in case there is a discrepancy.

What To Expect From A Home Inspection

A home inspection can unearth many problems you did not notice during your visits to the home. Typical findings include:

- Crumbling foundation
- Structural damage to floors, walls, and ceilings
- Water damage inside and outside the walls
- Termite damage
- Porch railings or posts in poor condition
- Heating and cooling systems need to be cleaned or do not work properly
- Roof needs repair
- Sinkholes

- Broken or leaking pipes
- Electrical wiring not functioning or broken
- Broken water fixtures or light fixtures
- Windows that do not open
- Uneven doorways
- Improper insulation
- Mold
- Water contamination
- Septic tank issues, or
- Hazardous chemicals

Most homes will only experience a few minor issues, but some older homes may have more problems than they are worth.

The damage to the homes could cost you thousands of dollars if you are unaware of the damage prior to purchasing the home.

While disclosure of some problems is mandatory, many homeowners do not even know that some of these problems exist until they try to sell their homes.

On the day of the inspection, you should expect to hear about some problems. You should be given a detailed report of the findings that will outline drastic problems and those that can be fixed easily.

Some lenders will not approve the home loan until the problems are fixed and another inspection is conducted.

Specific Places That Should Be Inspected

When interviewing home inspectors, make sure to ask whether the following areas are inspected:

- Chimney and fireplace
- Attic and basement
- Crawl space
- Swimming pools, and
- Smoke detectors and appliances

These are important areas that can be very costly to repair once you have purchased the home. Many homeowners are willing to replace a chimney cap or remove mold from the basement. You should make sure that these areas are inspected prior to the closing. You should also inspect these areas during the final walkthrough.

Chimney And Fireplace

Inspectors should be looking for:

- Missing, broken, or intact chimney caps
- Mortar between brick chimneys is intact
- Metal chimneys are not bent or contain holes and have all screws in place
- Creosote – this is buildup caused from wood burning fireplaces, and is flammable if not removed

Attic, Basement, And Crawl Spaces

Home inspectors should be on the lookout for the following:

- Mold
- Fire damage
- Rotting beams
- Insulation

- Damage from water, and
- Damage from animals and pests

Swimming Pools

When looking at the swimming pool, the inspector should look at the following:

- Swimming pool plumbing, and
- Swimming pool shell

Smoke Detectors And Appliances

- Make sure they work
- No leaks
- Check for broken hoses or connections
- Broken door handles
- Inadequate wiring

Termite Inspection

A termite inspection is a separate inspection that will give you an idea of structural damage to the home that has been caused by termites and other pests. This inspection is required by most lenders before they will guarantee you the money to purchase the home.

Termite inspections are not covered under the standard fee of a home inspection, so you may have to pay for the inspection unless the homeowners are willing to do so.

The inspection should take about an hour and will entail the inspector looking underneath siding, in basements, attics, and on the foundation of the home to see if there are termites present or if there are other insects such as ants, or fungus that are destroying the wood.

The inspector will also conduct an inspection inside the home as well. Since termites can live in different weather conditions, you should have the inspection done even if you live in an area that has lower temperatures than other regions.

Termites can be removed using an insecticide that is specially designed to kill termites and their eggs, but the damage left behind can be immense. If the home has been infested for a long time, then it may be beyond repair.

You will then have to discuss a reduction in price, repairs being made to the property, or walking away altogether.

How Homeowners Will React

How the homeowner will react to the results of the home inspection could determine whether you continue pursuing the home or whether you let it go and find another one.

Homeowners have their own agenda when it comes to selling their home. These include:

- Buying another home
- Moving to another state
- Using the money to pay for family medical emergencies
- Retirement, or
- Making money on an investment property

This means that there are varying degrees as to what they are willing to pay for and what they are not willing to pay for. If the homeowner is not in a rush to sell, then they may contest the findings and refuse to repair certain items. If they need to make as much money as possible, they may agree to lower the price a little or make repairs that cost the least on the list.

Homeowners know they are taking risks when selling older homes. But what about new homes? If your new home does not pass inspection, it is up to the builder to make the necessary repairs. You should make sure this is included in the contract before signing it.

If you are buying a home that homeowners have already moved out of, you may be able to get the repairs paid for without having to be too pushy.

If the homeowners are paying another mortgage, they are eager to sell and may opt to pay for the repairs upfront or give you a price reduction.

This will depend on the circumstances. There is always a certain amount of luck that goes into buying a home.

<u>Ways A Home Inspection Can Lower The Final Price</u>

Even though you will have to spend money upfront for a home inspection, you may save more money than you anticipated once the results come back. This is especially true for older homes or new homes that were not built using the right materials or according to safety codes.

There are a few ways you will be able to negotiate a lower price on the home before signing the final contracts.

- **Ask homeowners to make repairs**

This is the best way to save money on your new home. While you will not see a reduction in the final price of the home, you will not have to make as many repairs down the road. Also, you will not have to worry about the repairs once you have moved into the home.

While all homeowners are different, you should be aware that many do not want to make repairs unless the home absolutely cannot be sold in the condition it is in because it will endanger the new owners. Even minor repairs may pose a problem for homeowners. You should be firm, but friendly when negotiating this part of the contract. If you do not want to make these repairs and you strongly feel that the repairs should be made by the homeowner, you can still walk away from the home and find another.

You should give homeowners a week to think about making the repairs. Most homeowners will make their decision quickly because they want the sale to go through.

- **Ask homeowners for a price reduction**

If the homeowners do not want to spend money on the repairs that you have requested, they may agree to drop the final price of the home. While the price reduction will not be too drastic, any reduction is a good one since you will have to make the repairs yourself down the road.

If the homeowners suggest a reduction in the final price, you should consider the offer and find out how much the repairs will cost you. If it seems like a fair deal, then take it. If not, you can always ask for a larger reduction. Most buyers and sellers eventually agree on a price that will suit both parties.

- **Ask homeowners to pay for all closing costs**

  Another way to save money without relying on the homeowners to pay for the repairs is if they agree to pay the closing costs on both sides. This will free up some of your money so that you can make the repairs yourself.

  You may have to have a separate contract drawn up that will explain what the homeowners are responsible for paying, and what you are responsible for paying. This will make buying the home much easier.

  Any agreements that you make with the homeowners should be made in writing. Verbal agreements do not stand up in court, and are not common practice among real estate lawyers and agents when they are closing a deal. Your agent should make this clear to you at the beginning of the home buying process.

  Do not be discouraged if there seems to be a lot of paperwork. This is necessary and the usual standard practice for those who want to protect themselves from wrong doing and lawsuits later on.

The Final Walkthrough

On the day of the closing, you should have a final walkthrough whether you are purchasing a new home or an older home. Final walkthroughs are a way for you to determine if there is anything else you will need to discuss, get in writing, or have changed before you sign the paperwork.

The final walkthrough will include you, the homeowners, real estate agents, and if necessary, your lawyer. Unfortunately, many buyers skip the final walkthrough in anticipation of moving into the home quickly. But you should have one more walkthrough just to be sure.

The benefits of a final walkthrough include:

- Making sure all repairs that were conceded by the homeowners have been made
- Be sure additional repairs are not necessary
- Walls are intact
- Plumbing is intact
- Garage door opener
- Test doors and windows
- All appliances that were remaining are still in the home
- Appliances are in good working condition
- Electrical systems are working by turning on all lights

You will feel much better after the final walkthrough for many reasons. You will get to see firsthand the repairs that have been made, you will begin to see yourself living in the home, and you will be able to plan for the future in terms of what you want to keep in the home and what you want to remove.

In some cases, you will never meet the homeowners. If they have moved before putting the house on the market, you may be dealing directly with the homeowner's lawyer. It is still a good idea to ask questions about the home before signing the final paperwork.

The Closing

The closing is your last chance to ask for changes to the contract, to bring up any concerns, and to ask the homeowners any questions you may have about the home and the property.

At the closing, you should bring:

- A notepad
- Financial notes and mortgage approval paperwork
- Signed paperwork you have received over the course of the deal
- Identification, and
- The home inspection report

At this meeting, you will be signing the paperwork that will make the home yours. This is a very exciting time, but you should maintain your composure to make sure that you are getting what you are signing for. If repairs have not been made, then you have the option to wait until they are complete.

When To Walk Away

Any time after the home inspection if you begin to have doubts about purchasing the home, you should contact your real estate agent and voice your concerns.

Many first time homebuyers need reassurance that they are making the right decisions. Your real estate agent will want the sale to go through, but they know that there are other properties they can show you, so they are not really losing money if you decide to not buy the home.

There are many reasons to walk away from a home sale. These include:

- A bad report from the home inspector
- The homeowners are unwilling to pay for necessary repairs
- You find another home that suits your needs
- The price for the home is too high
- You decide you don't like the neighborhood
- Loss of your job, or

- A medical emergency

Walking away from a home is not giving up on your dream of homeownership. Unfortunately, there are times in life when buying a home is not possible. If the financial strain is going to be too much, for example, then you should seriously consider finding a lower priced home or a smaller home.

If you decide to walk away from a home, you should give yourself a few weeks to recuperate before going out there and finding another home. You should contact:

- The real estate agent
- The lender, or
- The builder

Let them know of your decision and that you will be in touch when the time is right. Many times after a bad report from a home inspector, it is just not worth spending the money on a home that will require a lot of repairs down the road. While all older homes will have some repairs, you should know the limits of what is acceptable and what will cost you too much money.

If you can get enough financing and you want to pursue the home regardless of the repairs that will have to be made, then go for it.

Sometimes buying an older home and fixing it up can be a fun activity for everyone involved. Only you can make these crucial decisions. A home inspection will help you realize how much work and money may be involved if you decide to purchase the home.

Chapter 5 - Financing Options

Financing your first home can be the most frustrating part of the home buying process. This is the time when you will figure out how to pay for the home. Most people have to take out a mortgage loan in order to afford the price. Which mortgage loans are right for you? How much of a down payment will be necessary? What is escrow?

You will have many questions about financing your first home. By knowing the facts, paying attention to interest rates, and looking into all of your mortgage options, you will be able to choose repayment terms that will fit your current income and allow you to safely make those monthly payments.

Types Of Home Loans

Deciding which home loan is the right one for you will depend on what you qualify for and what your lender is willing to give you. There are a few types of mortgage loans, including:

- Fixed rate mortgage loans
- Adjustable rate mortgage loans
- Balloon mortgages, and
- Jumbo loans

You should be familiar with these loans so that you will be able to make an informed decision when it comes to financing your new home.

Fixed Rate Mortgage Loans

For first time home buyers who are on a strict budget, choosing a fixed rate mortgage may be the loan for you. Your monthly payment will never change for the life of the loan because you will lock into the interest rate given at the time the loan was processed. You can take out loans that range from ten to thirty years.

There are many advantages to taking out mortgage loans that have fixed rates. You will be able to create a monthly budget for yourself, you will never be surprised by the amount you will have to pay each month, and you will be able to lock into a low interest rate.

The disadvantages may not mean much to you now, but as your family or your income grows, you may want to refinance and pay less each month so that you will be able to afford renovations, vacations, and other luxuries.

Since your mortgage is fixed, if interest rates drop, you will be trapped paying a higher rate. While you can refinance your mortgage, you will have to wait a certain amount of time, and even then there may be complications.

For those who have limited income, who have lower credit scores, or those who want the security of paying the same amount each month, then a fixed rate mortgage is the loan for you.

Adjustable Rate Mortgage Loans

If you expect to make more money in the next few years, and want to buy a bigger home, you may be interested in an adjustable rate mortgage. The major difference between an adjustable rate mortgage and a fixed rate mortgage is that the interest rate will vary year to year in an adjustable rate mortgage.

While the interest will be capped, you will still be paying more for each year that you own the home unless interest rates drop over an extended period of time. Most adjustable rate mortgages cannot be raised more than 2 interest points per year, and up to 7 points for the life of the loan.

These loans are good for those who want a larger home and who expect to increase their earning each year to afford the increase. If you are in a position to take out an adjustable rate mortgage, you will be able to lock into a fixed rate that may be lower than your original rate.

This is the main advantage of these loans. Most lenders will only give you two years to lock into a rate or the loan will remain adjustable for the life of the loan.

Balloon Mortgages

If you are only planning on living in your first home for a few years, usually five to seven, you may look into a balloon mortgage. These mortgages require that you pay them off in five to seven years. They have a lower interest rate that is fixed.

If after the term of the mortgage has passed and you want to remain in the home, you will have to refinance and choose a fixed rate or adjustable mortgage to pay off the existing mortgage, as balloon mortgages cannot be renewed.

Only consider this mortgage if you are planning on moving after a certain amount of time or if you think you can pay the mortgage off in that amount of time.

Jumbo Loans

Most first time home buyers will not need to take out a jumbo loan unless they are buying a very large home. These loans are valued over $275,000 and are used to purchase land and a home. More collateral will be needed in order to qualify for one of these loans. The interest rates are comparable to fixed and adjustable rate mortgages, and have the same payment terms.

Now that you know about the types of mortgages that are available, you should be thinking about which lender to use. With so many lenders out there, it may be difficult to sort through all of them and find the right one. Doing a little homework will help you get the lowest interest rate possible.

Where To Find A Lender

These days there are many places to find a mortgage lender, such as:

- Newspaper advertisements
- Television advertisements
- Family or friends
- Your Current lender
- Your Current bank, or
- Online

As you can see, finding a lender should not be too difficult. You may have to contact several lenders before you find a lender that will give you a loan that meets your needs. When you apply for a home mortgage loan, the lender will check the following:

- Your credit score
- Your credit history
- Your current income
- Income of co-signer
- References (professional and personal)
- Current interest rates based on the amount you are asking for
- Status of other loans you may have

- Number of years you have been eligible to work, and
- Number of years you have had credit

There are many factors that will go into your approval or denial of a home loan. You will have to be patient. You should contact a few lenders to see which ones will give you the best deal. Once the offers have been received, you will have to make some important decisions.

You should feel free to contact your lender at any time during the home buying process with questions and concerns you may have. Other important information the lender will need before granting you a loan include:

- The home inspection report
- The termite inspection report, and
- The home appraisal

These reports are very important to a lender because they will tell the lender how much the home is actually worth and the types of damage that have lowered the overall value of the property.

Lenders expect homeowners to remain in the home for at least five years. This will allow them to make a profit on the money they have loaned you. It is not worth it to them if you have to sell the home shortly after buying it because there is too much damage and you can no longer live there.

Applying For A Home Loan

When applying for a home loan, you will have to bring the information listed above to the lenders office, or if applying online, supply copies that are faxed to the lender. You will be asked additional questions that will help lenders determine if you are able to pay the loan back on time. These questions include:

- Number of years renting a home or apartment
- Late payments on credit cards and other loans
- Active loans (such as student loans or car loans)
- Number of years at your current job
- Additional income
- Amount of the loan and number of years to pay it back
- Number of years living in an area
- Dependents that are living at your home
- Tax returns and bank statements

Applying for a loan can take a week or more. This is because background checks, credit checks, and references must be checked first before the loan will be processed.

In the meantime, you should be concentrating on gathering your paperwork, calling friends and family that you want to use as references, and sorting through your papers in case you cannot find everything the lender requests.

If you do not have your back tax returns, you can contact the IRS and request them by year. Many times, lenders will need to see returns from at least three years ago. Bank statements and bill statements from the past year should be enough to secure a loan.

If you are turned down for a home loan, you will be notified as to the reasons why. This can be devastating, but you should find other lenders and try to apply again. If you have poor credit, you may need to go through a lender that specializes in granting loans to those with poor credit. You may have to pay a higher interest rate, but at least you will be granted a loan.

Reasons for possible denial include:

- Poor credit or not enough credit
- Length of time at your job is too short
- Income level for the amount of loan requested
- Loan default
- Failure to pay rent or other bills, or
- Too much credit

Applying for a home loan can be stressful, but if you have good credit, steady employment, and enough income, you should have little trouble qualifying for a loan.

What Not To Do When Applying For A Home Loan

There are a few things you should not do after applying for a home loan:

- Buy a new car
- Begin a new job
- Buy new furniture and other large items using your credit cards
- Apply for a credit card, or
- Default on student loans or other loans

All of these actions will cause your credit score to change which will give lenders an inaccurate view of your spending habits and your overall credit score. If you take a job that pays less than you noted on your home loan application, your lender may not agree to grant you the loan.

If possible, do not begin a new job until you have moved into your home. Try not to spend money on credit cards. Buy furniture and other items using cash, or wait until you have signed the final contract and are a homeowner.

Increase Your Chances For Approval

There are a few ways to increase your chances for loan approval that will also help you determine what you will be able to afford each month:

- *Pre-approval*

  Many experts agree that applying for a loan before you find a home and being pre-approved will help you create a budget, buy a home that is in your price range, and help lenders make their decisions faster.

- *Ask for only the amount you will need*

  One way to increase your chances for a home loan is to not ask for more than you will qualify for. This means you will have to look at your income level, the amount of debt you have, and the expected monthly mortgage payment. You should also factor in cost of living expenses, because your lender will. Apply for the amount you will need and nothing more.

- *Pay off credit cards*

  If you are thinking about buying a home in the next few years, you should prepare by paying off those credit cards and only using them for emergencies. Do not cancel your existing cards since this may actually lower your credit score. By showing you have a zero balance on your credit cards, you will be showing lenders that you know how to use credit wisely and you have been paying your cards off on time.

- *Always pay bills on time*

This includes your electric bill, rent, student loans, and other bills that you may have to pay each month. By creating a track record that can be traced, you will be showing lenders that you are a responsible person who deserves to have a home loan.

How Home Appraisals Can Affect Your Home Loan

Unfortunately, a home appraisal can affect the status of your loan. If the home appraisal comes under the selling price of the home, most lenders will not grant the loan. This can be heartbreaking, but there are a few solutions that may work depending on the rules of the lender. The following options are available:

The Homeowner Reduces The Selling Price

Depending on the appraised value in comparison to the asking price, some homeowners will be willing to lower the price of the home if they need to sell quickly.

You should not count on this happening since many homeowners want to receive the price they are asking for. You may have no choice but to find another home.

A Higher Down Payment

Some lenders will grant you the loan if you agree to pay a larger down payment on the home and assume the financial risk. This is only an option if you can afford to pay a larger down payment. Do not risk your financial security in these cases; it is just not worth it.

Dispute The Appraisal

You can send a letter to your lender disputing the appraisal or have another appraiser determine the value of the home. You will have to pay for this second appraisal, which may or may not yield the same results. There is no guarantee that your lender will accept the second appraisal.

Find Another Lender

This is a last resort move because it will postpone the closing for another month or so and there no guarantee that the lender will accept the appraisal.

Since home appraisals are required by most lenders, you should find out during the loan application process the policies that the lender has when dealing with appraisals. If your lender will not accept a lower selling price, you putting a larger down payment, or other solutions to a low appraisal, you should consider finding another lender just in case there are any problems down the road.

Home appraisals are based on the current value of homes in the neighborhood, homes that are comparable in size, the housing market, and the age of the home. While you can expect to hear different numbers from different appraisers, you will see that these numbers will usually not be too far off.

The only real benefit of a low home appraisal is that it will tell the homeowners to list the home for less money so that they will be able to sell it. In the meantime, you will have to find another home.

How Home Inspections Can Affect Your Home Loan

While a poor home inspection will usually not deter a lender from granting a home loan, you should be aware that some lenders will not grant a loan if there is termite damage or structural damage to the home due to water or age.

This will also lower the overall appraisal of the home, which could be another issue that lenders may have when deciding to approve a home loan.

If the home inspection is not favorable, ask your lender what will need to be done in order to rectify the problem. Many times removing the termites and correcting the water damage is all that will be needed. Many times homeowners will foot the bill for these types of repairs.

Additional Fees For Home Loans

You may notice that you will have to pay small fees throughout your home buying experience. It seems that every piece of paper you sign, file, or request will cost you some money. Here is a list of fees that you may be charged:

- Credit report fee
- Loan discount fee
- Lender's inspection fee
- Appraisal fee
- Loan origination fee
- Mortgage insurance application fee
- Assumption fee
- Hazard insurance
- Title search, and
- Title insurance

These fees can add up, so you will want to be prepared and have a little extra in savings for when these fees come up. Some of these fees can be put off until the closing, but you should be planning for them in advance.

Escrow And Other Loans Terms

As you are going through the home loan process, you will run across a few terms that you will not understand. You should ask your lender to explain these terms so that you will fully understand the type of loan you are applying for, the lenders policies, and other information that will be important throughout the life of the loan. Here are some common terms you may encounter:

- *Escrow*

  While this term can mean different things in different situations, you will see it often when closing on a home. If you place a down payment on a home, it will be in escrow until all the paperwork has been signed. The money is held by a neutral third party, such as another bank or escrow service, and will be distributed once the deal is over. You can ask your real estate agent about escrow services in your area.

- *Mortgage*

  Even though you have heard of a mortgage before, you probably thought of it as the home loan you will be paying once you move into your new home. Technically, a mortgage is a lien on your home created by your lender. If you cannot make payments on your home, the lender will have the right to sell the property in order to gain the money that they have lost.

- *Foreclosure*

  This is a term that refers to homes whose owners could not make payments each month. Once a lender has decided to sell the home, it will be in foreclosure. You should find out ways to work with your lender in case you miss a mortgage payment at any time. Having this knowledge in advance will make financial emergencies easier to deal with.

- *Mortgage Broker*

A mortgage broker is a person who does not work for a bank, but rather works on commission to match homebuyers with many lenders that may not be in your area. If you have poor credit, you may want to secure a home loan through a mortgage broker because you will have a better chance than going through a bank that only has one lender to choose from – themselves.

- *Points*

This refers to the interest rate on your loan. If you choose an adjustable rate loan, for example, your points may be capped each year so that they cannot exceed a certain number.

- *Down Payment*

A down payment is helpful in several ways. It will lower the amount of money you will need for a home loan, it will allow lenders to see that you are responsible for paying off a mortgage, and it will move the home buying process faster. Most first time homeowners will put down no more than 20% for a down payment.

You do not want to overextend yourself by putting a huge down payment on a home because you may not have enough money to pay your mortgage, afford new furniture, or make home repairs.

- *Debt to Income Ratio*

This is one way that lenders will sue to determine if you can afford your monthly mortgage payments on your current income. The lender will subtract all your reoccurring debt to determine how much is left for a mortgage payment.

This is why not buying a car or spending money on your credit cards is so important when buying a home. The less debt you have will mean more available money for your mortgage payment.

- *Private Mortgage Insurance*

If you cannot afford to put down more than 5% on a home, you may not be approved for a loan. But if you purchase private mortgage insurance, your lender may agree to give you the loan. This extra insurance will protect the lender in case you default on the loan by paying them at least 15% of the total loan value. This will cost you a little extra each month, but it may be worth it.

- *Credit Report*

Before you apply for a home loan, you should obtain copies of your credit report so that you can check for errors; see how much money you owe on credit cards and loans, and to see what your credit score is. This is another way that lenders will determine if you will receive a loan.

There are three credit reports that you should obtain, because you will not know which one the lender will base their decisions on.

Chapter 6 - Making an Offer

By this point, you should have found a real estate agent, contacted a few lenders, and seen a few homes. If you have not made up your mind on a home yet, you should take your time and keep looking. But keep in mind that if you wait too long, you may end up in a bidding war with another buyer.

Making an offer on a home is a huge step. You will be taking on the responsibility of a mortgage, repairs, lawn care, and other chores that homeowners sometimes gripe too much about.

While you should be cautious, you should also make a bid on a home that you really like within a week after seeing it. This will put your mind at ease so that you can think of all the other items you will have to get done before the closing.

What To Do Before Making An Offer

Before you make an offer on a home, you should do the following:

- Attend open houses
- Find out more about a property
- Find out about taxes in the area, and
- Have an appraisal done before making an offer

These suggestions will help you make the most informed decision possible when it comes to buying your first home.

Attend Open Houses

Attend as many open houses as you can in homes that are in the area where you want to live. This will give you the opportunity to see what's out there, the going price of homes in the area, and also give you a basis of comparison when looking at other homes.

Open houses are fun because you will be able to look into every area of the home without having to worry about the homeowners and real estate agents following you around. Many times, you may even find your new home this way.

Almost every weekend in most neighborhoods, there will be an open house. Stop by and see for yourself what the homes in the area look like and what you can get for your budget.

Find Out More About A Property

If you find a home that you might want to buy, you should find out everything you can about the property first before making an offer. Visit the county clerk's office or land records office to see how much the current homeowners paid for their land and the value of their property.

This will give you an idea of how much you should offer for the home. If the home is in an area that has seen better days, then you can make an offer that is less because when you sell the property someday, you may have to lower your price as well.

Find Out More About Taxes In The Area

As a homeowner, you will be paying yearly property taxes, local taxes, school taxes, community dues, and other taxes that could drive your household spending through the roof. Before you commit to living in a certain area, make sure you understand everything you will be paying each year.

Your real estate agent should have the neighborhood information that will help you decide where you want to move. You can also visit your local tax office and see how much the current homeowners paid in taxes last year.

Have An Appraisal Done Before Making An Offer

Most first time home buyers do not have an appraisal done until their lender asks them for one. But you are well within your rights to ask for a home appraisal before making an offer. You will not have to share the findings with anyone until your lender asks to see the appraisal.

How To Write A Purchase Offer

This is the most important step when making an offer to buy your first home. The purchase offer should outline everything you expect from the homeowner and what they can expect from you. You should include the following in your offer:

- price being offered
- amount of deposit on the home
- amount of money you will be putting down on the home
- mortgage terms
- Contingencies (such as appliances that will stay repairs that will need to be made, removal of items in the yard, etc.)
- when closing will take place
- specify who will pay which fees
- any reports that will be needed, and

Each of these categories should be explained in its own paragraph. You should try to be as specific as possible when writing up a purchasing offer.

Each state has its own laws concerning contingency, amount of time a buyer has to respond to the offer, and fees that are to be paid. Be aware of these laws before sending your offer or you may end up with a counter offer or a rejection.

Have a lawyer or your real estate agent look over the purchase offer before sending it. They may have some advice or additional categories you should add depending on the age of the home, the neighborhood, and the laws that exist. If you make an offer that is reasonable, well written, and hard to break, then you will be on your way to buying a home.

Making An Offer

After completing your research, you will be ready to make an offer on your first home. You will have to visit your real estate agent to sign a formal agreement that will outline your offer and for how long you will be making this offer. Most agreements will give sellers three days to a week to consider the offer.

In this time, the offer may be accepted, rejected, or a counter offer will be made. You will have to decide what you will want to do next if the offer is rejected or another offer is made. If the offer is accepted, then you will have to contact your lender, a home inspector, and make arrangements for your move.

Most homes will go to closing within a month after an offer has been accepted. This may seem like a long time, but it is not. You will have plenty to do in the meantime.

Low Or High Offers

Hopefully, by researching the neighborhood, the property, and the value of the home, you will be able to come as close to the seller's price as possible.

Sometimes, though, this is not possible. There may be circumstances that may prohibit you from making an offer that is close to the selling price.

Making The Right Offer

The closer you can come to the asking price, the better off you will be. Once the home inspection is complete, the homeowners may have to come down in price anyway because of the repairs they will have to make.

Making the right decisions when buying a home are not always made quickly. You should play by the rules and just see what happens. If you get into a bidding war and cannot bid any higher, then it is best to let the home go and find another. You should not be a slave to your first home by buying one that is over your budget. There are many homes available if you keep looking.

How To Handle A Counter Offer And Offer Rejection

Sometimes, if you give homeowners an offer that is lower than their asking price, they may offer a counter offer. This is usually an offer that is more than your offer, but a little less than the asking price.

Counter Offer

Depending on where you live, the laws pertaining to counter offers will vary. Typically, the number of counter offers is limitless, but no counter offer can be the same. While counter offers are usually concerning money, these offers may also contain the following:

- Ownership of appliances
- Repairs
- Time frames for closing, and

- Time frames for counter offers

Buyers and sellers may only have hours to accept, reject, or offer another counter offer after receiving one. This can be a very stressful process, especially if you are dealing with a seller that has other offers on the table. While most homeowners will reject an offer if it is too low or they have received another, some will try to get the most they can from the sale which can include the smallest items in the home.

If you are determined to buy a home, but still want a lower price after the buyer has reacted with a counter offer, you can try to find a price that will suit everyone's needs. If you are making a counter offer that does not make that much of a difference, you should weigh the odds that another offer has been made, the homeowner will reject your offer, and that time is ticking for everyone.

Try your best to accept the counter offer before making one of your own. Is it really worth losing your dream home over one or two thousand dollars?

Dealing With Rejection

The hardest part about an offer rejection is that the homeowner does not have to answer your offer. If you do not hear from the homeowner within a week, it is safe to assume they are not interested in your bid. While this can be frustrating, you will have to move on. Begin your house hunting again and try to stay positive.

If the homeowner gives you a response in the form of a rejection, they may site the reason why in the paperwork. If your offer was too low, they had another offer, decided not to sell, or want to wait for a higher offer, at least you can move on without wondering why your bid was rejected.

Considering Items In The Home

When you are writing your purchase offer, you should consider the items that you would like to keep and items you would like to have removed from the home. These items can include:

- Certain appliances (such as the washer and dryer)
- Lighting fixtures
- Storage fixtures
- Single air conditioning units that fit into windows
- Hardware from windows and doors, or
- Pools

You should put these items in writing so that you will get them with the home. Some homeowners may try taking certain items with them either because they didn't know that you wanted them or because they were not supposed to be sold with the home to begin with. Be sure to obtain a list of items the homeowner is selling with the home so that you can compare it to your list.

This can also work in reverse. If there are items that you would like removed from the home or the property before you move in, you should specify these in the offer.

Understanding The Seller

One of the key elements of making a solid offer is having an understanding of the seller. Your real estate agent will be able to tell you a little about the seller that may help when trying to come up with a fair offer.

When deciding on an offer for the home, you should find out the following about the seller:

- How eager are they to sell their home?
- How long have they lived in the home?
- How many offers have they received?
- How many have they turned down?
- Have they lowered their asking price?
- Are they relocating to another area?
- Do they need to sell their home quickly?
- Are they waiting for their asking price?

These questions, although you may not know the answer to some of them, will help you make an offer that will be looked at by homeowners and taken seriously. Sometimes when a homeowner needs to leave the area in a certain amount of time they will lower their asking price. This could be an advantage for you, but if the homeowners have already lowered the price, they may not want to lower it any further.

Make a reasonable offer and see what happens. Depending on the circumstances, it may be accepted.

What To Do In A Buyer's Market

In a buyer's market, you will have more choices when it comes to the types of homes you can purchase. Depending on how long the market favors the buyer, you will also have the luxury of taking your time because bidding wars are much less. When buying your first home, you should check out all your options. That home you couldn't afford a few years ago may be in your price range today.

When looking for a home in a buyer's market, you should do the following:

- Stay current with the listings in your area

- Sign up for free email listings and newsletters
- Check out homes that have recently been reduced
- When making an offer, ask for closing fees to be paid for by the seller
- See if there are other offers, such as appliances that come with the home
- Ask for certain allowances (carpeting, roofing, siding, ect.)
- Do not be afraid to offer a lower price, and
- Ask for a shorter response time

In a buyer's market, homeowners may offer these options to you as incentive to buy their homes. They may also offer warranties on appliances that you should take advantage of.

There are dangers that you should consider when buying in a buyer's market, however.

- If you are not planning on living in the home for more than three years, you may want to wait until the market changes or plan to live in the home longer. Many times, market trends can last for a few years. If you need to move after a year or so, you may have difficulty finding a buyer and you may have to sell the home for less than what you paid for it.

- While most homeowners stay in their homes for at least two years in order to save money in taxes, marketing trends have been known to last longer. You should be prepared for this when buying your first home.

- Make sure a thorough home inspection has been completed before buying the home. If you decide you cannot live there after you have bought the property, you may have difficulty selling it and you will have to spend more money making repairs.

Even though you cannot predict how the market will change, you should consider a home that you can afford, that you will want to live in for a long time, and one that can be improved upon while you own it.

What To Do In A Sellers Market

In a seller's market, you will have to play the game slightly different than you would in a buyer's market. In this type of market, there are many buyers who will want to buy homes that are attractive and priced within their budget. Homeowners will have their pick of offers to choose from so your offer will have to stand out in more than just price.

When looking for a home in a seller's market, you should:

- Make an offer that is close to the asking price or slightly over
- Send a pre-qualification letter from your lender with the offer
- Choose a closing date that is sooner rather than later
- Do not ask for too many contingencies
- Send a personal letter
- Promise more of a down payment, and
- Use a real estate agent that gets things done quickly

In a seller's market, you may also want to think about the dangers of buying a home. If you make an offer that is too high and you find out later on that the mortgage payments will be a struggle, you may have to sell. Depending on changes in the market, this may be more difficult than when you were looking for a home.

Buying your first home during this time may also be difficult because you will not be able to put much down, you may only qualify for a certain amount of money which may not be enough to compete during a bidding war, and you may be out bid by those who have more experience than you do.

When you decide to buy a home, you should be looking at your finance situation, the market, and the asking price for the homes you are interested in making an offer on.

If you can wait a few months to see where the market is headed, then maybe this is the best way to save more money and find a home that is affordable. This is a waiting game that no one wants to play, but may be necessary, especially if this is your first home purchase.

Seller's markets and buyer's markets have their advantages and disadvantages, but in the end, the offer that you make will determine whether your offer will be accepted.

Chapter 7 – Closing the Deal

Drawing up contracts, having the final walkthrough, and going to the closing are the last steps you will have to take when buying your first home. This is the time when having a real estate agent you can trust, and a little knowledge of home buying comes in handy.

What about all of those other miscellaneous fees that will come up before and during the closing? You should be aware of additional fees when you apply for a loan and when you are closing on your new home.

Contracts

Your purchase offer was the first contract you will be involved in when you want to buy a home. You should refer to this contract during the closing period to make sure that your rights are covered and that you are getting everything you pay for.

By writing a solid purchase offer that outlines what you want from the homeowners, you will be protected in case of disagreements and other issues before closing. But a purchase offer is just one of many pieces of paper you will have to see and sign before you can move into your home. Other contracts include:

- Contingencies
- Builder contracts
- Mortgage contracts, and
- Closing agreements

These contracts may vary in length depending on the forms being used and the information that will have to be included.

Contingencies

Real estate contingencies can be added onto an existing contract or can be created as a separate contract depending on what you would like to include in the purchase offer. Contingencies can include a wide range of items, including:

- Home inspections and pest inspections
- Home appraisals
- Financing
- Septic system tests
- Appliances that will stay in the home, and
- Property surveys

Contingencies can make or break a sale, so you should be sure to use the correct forms when filing contingencies and to word them correctly.

You will need to include a resolution for repairs that may need to be done before you can move into the home. If it is agreed upon in writing that the homeowners will take care of all or some repairs that may be found during a home inspection, this will save time later on.

You should also include ways to get out of the deal that include loan denial, repairs that cannot be fixed, and lead, mold, or radon that is found in the home. Having a way out of the contract will save you money and time.

If you are buying a home that is for sale by owner, you should find an attorney or real estate agent that is willing to help you create a contingency list and edit it where necessary. Do not rely on the seller's agent because they are after their client's best interests and not yours.

Builder Contracts

If you are buying a new home from a builder, you will have to sign a builder's contract that states you have the financial means to pay for a new home, that you have decided on a location for your new home, and that you are ready to build.

You should hire an attorney at this point to go over the contract to see if there are any problems that will have to be ironed out before you begin building the home.

Mortgage Contracts

In order to complete your home buying, you will have to be approved for a mortgage by a lender and you will have to sign a contract in which you agree to an interest rate, monthly payment schedule, rate plan, down payment, and other fees.

These contracts are standard loan contracts that will explain the consequences of not paying your mortgage. You should read this paperwork carefully before signing anything.

Closing Agreements

These are the final contracts you will have to sign before you get the keys to your new home. You should read this paperwork carefully and be prepared to pay any closing costs at this time.

Home Warranties

If you are buying an older home, you may want to purchase a home warranty that will cover repairs that will have to be made during your first year of ownership.

While a home inspection will catch any immediate repairs, no one can foresee an oven falling apart or a dryer burning out. Since you may not have a lot of extra money left over after paying for closing costs, down payment, and mortgage payments, having extra insurance will allow you to make the repairs you will need.

Most policies will cost between three-hundred and five-hundred dollars. Coverage will begin the day of your closing and will last for a year. You will have the option of renewing the policy if you would like at that time. If you need to have an appliance repaired, you may have to pay small co-pay at the time of the repair.

Not all policies are the same, so you should do your research to find the best deal. Compare the types of repairs that are covered under the policies and choose the one that fits your home.

Closing

When you finally arrive at the closing, you should expect to:

- Sign contracts
- Do a final walkthrough
- Pay closing costs, and
- Get your keys

The closing can take an hour or two, but usually moves quickly because there is little left to do. At the closing you will probably meet the homeowners. This could be the first time you will meet them. This is a good time to ask if there is anything about the home you will need to know.

Sign Contracts

When you sign contracts, read them carefully to make sure everything that has been discussed is in the contract. Ask questions that you may have at this time.

Final Walk Through

The final walkthrough of the home will take place before or during the closing. This is the final chance for you to see the home before it becomes yours. Make sure the items on your contingency are in place so that you can sign the contracts.

Paying Closing Costs

Typically, the buyer will have to pay the closing costs associated with buying a home. But in a buyer's market, you may be able to add a contingency that states the seller will be responsible for all costs. This may appeal to sellers who want to sell their home quickly.

When deciding who should pay the closing costs, you should research laws that may be in place that dictate who pays for what. Many times, buyers and sellers will agree to split all costs including closing, home inspection, pest inspection, and home appraisal costs. You will have to negotiate with the sellers to see which you will be responsible for.

Get Your Keys

After signing the contracts, you will receive the keys to your new home. This is an exciting feeling and one that will be with you for a long time!